Sandwiches in space

Hello, I'm Messy.
What's your name?

My name is ....

Thames & Hudson

Let's go to OKIDO!

Are you looking for adventure?
Is there something you need to know?
Come on, let's go to OKIDO!

Messy Monster

Zoe  **Felix**

Messy's best friends

Find Foxy

Where is Foxy hiding in the story?

A clue – look somewhere rocky and far away.

Zim
A super scientist

Zam
A great inventor

Zoom
A morphing master

One night Messy found his friends Zoe and Felix gazing at the sky. They spotted a shooting **star**.

The star grew closer
and closer until it landed
on the ground with a
crash.

It looked like a rock. Messy gave it a big lick and two eyes popped open! When Messy asked its name, the rock answered in **squeaks** and **beeps**, so he just called it Pebble.

They all jumped in Okidoodle and set off to visit Zim, Zam and Zoom at their lab.

Brrrrrmmm!

Pebble's strange language

Let's ski-doodle, Okidoodle!

Zim and Zam did some tests on Pebble. Zoom's scan showed that she was full of **cheese**.

Pebble was a baby moon rock!

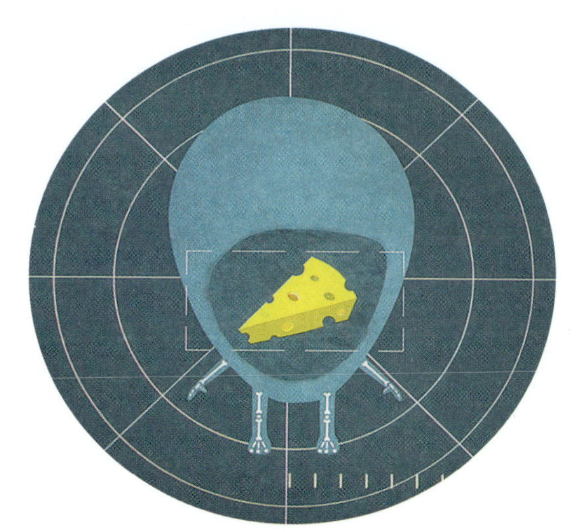

You'll have to take her home.

But where are we going to get a rocket?

Zim led them to a huge launch pad. In the middle stood a brand-new rocket. Pebble, Messy, Zoe and Felix jumped on board.

3... 2... 1...

BLAST OFF!

All the excitement made Messy hungry. He took out a sandwich, but it floated away before he could eat it. When Messy tried to catch it, he **floated** too!

Zoe called ground control.

Zim explained that **gravity** is the stuff that pulls things to the ground on Earth. There is less gravity in space, so things float.

The rocket landed on the Moon and everyone stepped outside. This time they didn't float, they **bounced**. It was like being on a trampoline! Zoe called Zim on her communicator.

Zim, why are we bouncing on the Moon? OVER.
It's because on the Moon there is enough gravity to stop you floating, but not enough to stick you to the ground. OVER.

The three friends were so busy **bouncing**, they forgot all about their mission. Then Messy noticed that Pebble had disappeared.

They turned to look at the rocks and lots of beady eyes blinked back at them! Messy tried being friendly, but the rocks just stared at him blankly.

Suddenly, Pebble appeared, **jumping** up and down between two big moon rocks. She had found her family!

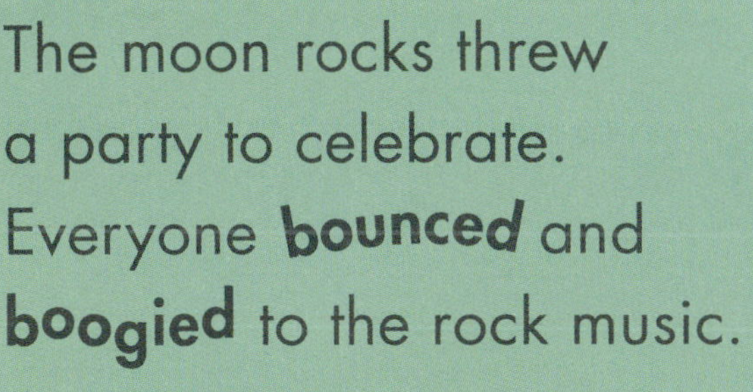

The moon rocks threw a party to celebrate. Everyone **bounced** and **boogied** to the rock music.

BA-BA-BA-DOOBIE-WAH!

Let's party!

Mission accomplished!
Messy and his friends
waved goodbye to Pebble
and zoomed back to OKIDO.
Whoooosh!

When they stepped off the rocket,
it felt good to stick to the ground again.
Suddenly, Messy's tummy gave a loud **rumble!**

The end

What is gravity?

Gravity is the stuff that pulls things to the ground on Earth. Without it we would float off into space!

Wow! Gravity is invisible and really strong.

There is hardly any **gravity** in space, so things float.

There is not enough **gravity** on the Moon to stick you to the ground, but there is enough to stop you floating.

Zam's workshop

You can't see or feel **gravity**, but you can watch it working. Try this!

Find a pebble. Hold it up and let go. It falls to the ground. **That's gravity!**

Add stickers of Messy and his friends floating in space!

Giggle with the gang!

Have you heard about the cow astronaut?

It landed on the Moooooon!

How do you get a baby astronaut to sleep?

You rock-et!

First published in the United Kingdom in 2015 by Thames & Hudson Ltd, 181A High Holborn, London WC1V 7QX

Licensed by Doodle Productions Limited based on the TV series 'Messy Goes to OKIDO'

Printed and bound in China by Toppan Leefung Printing Limited

British Library Cataloguing-in-Publication Data
A catalogue record for this book is available from the British Library

ISBN 978-0-500-65062-2

To find out about all our publications, please visit **www.thamesandhudson.com**. There you can subscribe to our e-newsletter, browse or download our current catalogue, and buy any titles that are in print.